Direct Energy Weapons

The Great Reset is On Fire

Your life is at risk

Christofer Parson - 2023
A Waimea publication
Hardcover Premium Edition
ISBN: 9798859072781

*Mountain **DEW**, the US Brand,*

*made a drink called **Maui Blast***

Pineapple flavor

The Mystery of Maui's Inferno

666 degrees

Everything Burns Except the Trees and the Blue stuff:

DEW?

Copyright © 2023 Christofer Parson

All rights reserved. No part of this publication may be reproduced, distributed, or transmitted in any form or by any means, including photocopying, recording, or other electronic or mechanical methods, without the prior written permission of the publisher, except in the case of brief quotations embodied in critical reviews and certain other noncommercial uses permitted by copyright law.

Created in Waimea, Hawaii

*In the whispers of the gentle winds and the rhythmic dance of the Pacific waves, Maui echoes the ancient tales of Mother Earth. This sacred isle, wrapped in emerald and azure, is not merely a piece of land; it's a **<u>living energy portal</u>**, breathing testament to the universe's vibrant soul.*

The energy of Maui beckons us, urging humanity to tune into a higher frequency, to align ourselves with the vibrations of the cosmos. To truly honor Maui, and by extension our planet, we must commit to elevating our collective consciousness. In our every thought, word, and deed, let us resonate with respect, compassion, and understanding.

Now, more than ever, the call is clear and urgent: It's time. Time to recognize the profound interconnectedness of all life, to cherish the delicate balance that sustains us. Time to not just exist, but to truly live, in harmony with the Earth and her endless wonders.

Time to wake up

As we mourn, let us remember that what we perceive as death is but an illusion. Souls, timeless and eternal, merely transition, echoing the endless cycle of rebirth.

For in the spirit of Maui lies the heart of the world. And in answering its call, we find our own true selves.

Let us rise. Let us remember. Let us resonate

The Mystery of Maui's Inferno - Everything Burns Except the Trees:

DEW ? DIRECT ENERGY WEAPONS
Your life is at Risk

TABLE OF CONTENT

Introduction   page 12

The Mysterious Power of DEWs: Melting Metal, Sparing Trees

Chapter 1 : Be ready for the unthinkable   page 14

Chapter 2: Basic Principles of DEWs   page 18

2.1 Understanding Directed Energy

2.2 Energy vs. Kinetic Attack

2.3 Types of Energy Used

2.4 Energy Transmission and Focus

2.5 Power Sources and Storage

2.6 Targeting and Guidance Systems

2.7 Effects on Targets

2.8 Challenges and Limitations

Chapter 3: Historical Development and Milestones of DEWs   page 22

3.1 Early Conceptualizations

3.2 The Birth of Lasers

3.3 Microwave Technology

3.4 Sonic and Ultrasonic Weapons

3.5 The Evolution of DEWs: Key Milestones

3.6 International Collaborations and Tensions as DEW Race Intensifies

3.7 Current Leaders in DEW Research

Chapter 4: Modern Applications and Implications of DEWs

page 29

4.1 Defense and Strategic Uses

4.2 Civilian and Law Enforcement Applications

Bridging the Lethality Gap
Active Denial Systems (**ADS**)
Crowd Control: A Shift from Physical to Directed Force
Perimeter Defense: Keeping Intruders at Bay
Wildlife Deterrence: A Novel Application

4.3 Space Applications

4.4 Technological Disruption and Countermeasures

4.5 Environmental Implications

4.6 Ethical and Legal Debates

4.7 Economic Impact

Chapter 5: DEWs in the Global Landscape page 35

5.1 Global Proliferation and DEW Development

5.2 The Diplomacy of DEWs

5.3 Potential Flashpoints and Geopolitical Implications

5.4 DEWs and the New Arms Race

5.5 International Treaties and Regulatory Challenges

5.6 Collaborative Research and Shared Concerns

5.7 The Role of Non-State Actors

Chapter 6: Looking Ahead - DEWs in the Future and the Maui Event of August 2023   **page 39**

6.1 The Technological Evolution of DEWs

6.2 Economic and Industrial Growth

6.3 **The Maui Event of August 2023**

6.4 Military and DEWs

6.5 Environmental and Space Considerations

6.6 Strategies for Global Cooperation

6.7 Envisioning the 2030 Landscape

Chapter 7: Countermeasures and Defense Against DEWs

                               page 45

7.1 Understanding the DEW Threat Spectrum : Blue.

7.2 Traditional Defense Mechanisms

7.3 The Role of Materials Science

7.4 Electronic and Cyber counter mesures

7.5 Tactical Approaches and Training

7.6 Public and Civilian Defense

7.7 Reflecting on the Aluminum Question

Chapter 8: Ethical, Legal, and Humanitarian Implications of DEWs   page 69

8.1 The Double-Edged Sword: DEWs as Tools of Precision

8.2 DEWs and International Humanitarian Law

8.3 Human Rights Concerns and DEWs

8.4 The Accountability Gap

8.5 Psychological Impacts of DEWs on Soldiers and Civilians

8.6 Ethical Implications for Developers and Engineers

8.7 Pathways Forward: Balancing Innovation and Responsibility

Chapter 9: DEWs as Catalysts for Urban and Geographical Transformation: Maui's Pioneering Journey   **page 71**

9.1 Harnessing DEWs for Civilian Infrastructure

9.2 Maui: The Visionary Blueprint - Smart cities

9.3 Power and Energy Distribution

9.4 Communication Systems Reinvented

9.5 Urban Mobility and Traffic Management

9.6 Environmental Stewardship with DEWs

9.7 Challenges, Lessons, and the Path Ahead for Maui

**Conclusion:
Envisioning the Future with Directed Energy Weapons
page 77**

Introduction: Directed Energy Weapons - 3 Ps
A Fusion of Power, Precision, and Potential

<u>**The Great Reset has begun**</u>. **Waimea's waves know.**. In the realm of science fiction, energy-based weapons have consistently captured our imagination, evoking images of futuristic landscapes dominated by advanced civilizations with power at their fingertips. But what if this fiction is closer to reality than we thought? You might be the target. Read between the lines.

When you witness scenes of devastated areas where houses are reduced to rubble but trees stand untouched, as seen in Maui, or observe the curious phenomenon of metal melting while nearby wood remains unaffected, the science behind it becomes a topic of intrigue. **Consider this: Aluminium starts to melt at approximately 660.3°C (1220.54 degrees Fahrenheit) , while wood catches fire around 565°C. If a blast of heat can melt metal, what kind of technology can channel such precision?** Now, you know the answer: **Directed Energy Weapons** (DEWs).

<u>**DEW**s are advanced technological systems that emit energy in the desired direction without requiring a projectile.</u> Using lasers, microwaves, and other forms of energy, they deliver focused energy to their targets. The remarkable heat they can generate is beyond traditional sources' capabilities, especially in such a directed and controlled manner. This capability, underscored by the unusual events of **metals melting** while organic materials like wood remain untouched, exemplifies the power and potential of these weapons. They had already been tested before August 2023.

But it's not all about raw power. The emergence of **DEW**s signifies a paradigm shift in defense, warfare, and even potential civilian applications. Their precision, speed, and capability to tackle multiple threats simultaneously make them "formidable" assets when use peacefully. Yet, with immense power comes immense responsibility and myriad questions. How do they function? What are their warfare and defense implications? Can they be integrated into our daily lives, like in new infrastructure projects such as the Neom project in Saudi Arabia? Most importantly, how does one counteract them?

This concise book delves into the world of **DEW**s, exploring their mechanics, history, potential, and the challenges they pose for humanity. Throughout the chapters, you'll uncover answers, insights, and perhaps more questions as we shed light on the intricate relationship between science, ethics, and innovation that **DEW**s represent.

Prepare to traverse a riveting journey from fictional realms to the very boundaries of our current scientific reality in front of your eyes. Read between the lanes.

Chapter 1: Be ready for the unthinkable: 666°C

As we navigate the annals of **DEW**s, one cannot help but be awed by the amalgamation of science, engineering, and strategic vision that brought them into existence. While it's tempting to regard **DEW**s as mere technological innovations, they are the pinnacle of centuries of scientific endeavor. Every discovery, from rudimentary understandings of light and sound waves to sophisticated quantum physics and advanced material science, has contributed to their evolution.

Consider the journey of the humble laser. Its inception began well before its actual invention, anchored in the foundational exploration of light by pioneers like **Sir Isaac Newton and James Clerk Maxwell**. The 20th century saw **Albert Einstein** offer revolutionary insights into light's Quantum nature, setting the stage for the first laser in 1960. Fast-forward a few decades, and lasers have evolved from cutting tools and medical instruments to powerful defense/attacks assets for many nations.

This narrative is common for most **DEW**s: born from a mix of pure scientific curiosity and the urgent needs of geopolitics and defense. In this delicate balance, a recurring motif emerges—the double-edged sword of technological progress. DEWs promise precision and fewer unintended casualties, hinting at a more humane approach to warfare. Yet, they also introduce challenges, as their accessibility might lead to increased proliferation among diverse actors. Their silent and often unseen operations might stretch the limits of international laws and conventions.

While **DEW**s' underlying technology might seem distant, its implications are profoundly felt in the tangible spheres of strategy, diplomacy, and economics. Investments in DEW research highlight a country's military and technological ambitions. As nations like the **US, Russia, and China** lead the charge, **DEW**s become symbols of technological mastery and geopolitical strength.

However, amongst the whirlwind of strategy and technology, the human element persists. Innovations in **DEW**s are the product of countless scientists, engineers, and strategists tirelessly challenging the boundaries of possibility. Their challenges span beyond the technical to encompass moral and ethical dilemmas. How can the power of **DEW**s be harnessed responsibly? How can a balance between progress and restraint be achieved?

In subsequent chapters, we'll address these questions and more. From understanding the intricate workings of **DEW**s to grasping their global political implications, this exploration is both enlightening and crucial. As we approach a new defense and warfare era, understanding DEWs becomes indispensable for those invested in global peace and security.

The dawn of the DEW era is not merely a technological revolution; it is a sociopolitical and cultural shift for the best and the worst. As we peer into the vast expanse of possibilities these weapons present, it becomes evident that our approach to global defense, diplomacy, and even societal norms is set to undergo significant transformation.

Beyond the battlegrounds, the introduction of **DEW**s prompts reevaluation of several long-standing doctrines. Traditional warfare had clear demarcations—battlefields, uniforms, and discernible weapons. However, with **DEW**s' ability to strike discreetly, perhaps from thousands of miles away or even from the silent expanse of space, these boundaries become blurred. What then constitutes an act of aggression? **How do nations react to threats that may not be immediately visible or even discernible?**

The proliferation of DEWs also presents unique challenges in arms control. International treaties, like the Outer Space Treaty, may need revisiting and reinterpretation in the light of these advancements. The silent and often untraceable nature of **DEW** engagements could lead to situations where attribution becomes a challenge, raising the specter of conflicts without clear beginnings or resolutions.

Yet, for all the challenges they pose, **DEW**s also present "opportunities". Their precision offers the potential to minimize civilian casualties, shifting warfare paradigms from large-scale destruction to focused engagements. In domains like space, where debris from kinetic engagements can pose long-lasting hazards, **DEW**s can offer cleaner alternatives.

Economic and industrial sectors too are poised to feel the ripples of this evolution. The research, development, and deployment of **DEW**s will necessitate massive investments and could drive innovations in ancillary sectors like power storage, optics, and materials science. Regions and countries that become hubs for **DEW** research might see economic boons, much like the Silicon Valley explosion due to the tech industry.

In parallel, as **DEW**s permeate our collective consciousness, they will undoubtedly find their way into popular culture—films, literature, and art. Such mediums will play a pivotal role in shaping public perception, much like how nuclear weapons during the Cold War era influenced generations of thought and artistic expression.

But as we ponder the vast expanse of implications, at the heart remains an immutable truth—the essence of human decision-making. **DEW**s, in all their technological grandeur, are but tools. Their use, misuse, or restraint will be determined by human choices, guided by a complex matrix of morality, strategy, ambition, and fear. As we delve deeper into this world of directed energy, it is this human element that we must never lose sight of. For in our hands lies not just the power of advanced weaponry, but the weighty responsibility of wielding it judiciously.

In the forthcoming sections, we will embark on a comprehensive exploration, delving into the mechanics, the dark strategies, the ethics, and the broader societal implications of **DEW**s. Through this lens, we hope to present a holistic view, one that is not just technical but also deeply introspective, beckoning readers to reflect on our collective future in this weird new world.

Chapter 2: Basic Principles of DEWs
2.1 Understanding Directed Energy
Directed energy, in its most basic form, refers to the concentration of energy onto a specific target without the use of a projectile. This can be visualized as the difference between throwing a stone at a target (projectile-based) versus focusing a magnifying glass under the sun to burn a piece of paper (directed energy). **It's a high frequency device melting all the metals.**

2.2 Energy vs. Kinetic Attack
Traditional weapons, like bullets or missiles, rely on their mass and speed to deliver damage—this is a kinetic approach. **DEW**s, in contrast, leverage energy forms like light, sound, or electromagnetic waves to engage targets. Understanding this difference is fundamental to grasping why **DEW**s hold such promise and also why they pose unique challenges.

2.3 Types of Energy Used
DEWs can harness multiple forms of energy:
Electromagnetic Spectrum: Includes radio waves, microwaves, and lasers. Each frequency range within this spectrum can be utilized for different applications, from disrupting electronics to causing heat-based damage.
Acoustic Energy: Uses sound waves, typically outside the range of human hearing, to affect targets. While not as common as electromagnetic DEWs, acoustic weapons have potential applications in crowd control or underwater warfare.

2.4 Energy Transmission and Focus

One of the standout capabilities of Directed Energy Weapons (DEWs) is their ability to accurately deliver energy across extensive distances with minimal dispersion. This is a crucial feature for applications ranging from anti-missile systems to remote drone disruption. Here are some factors that play a vital role:

Beam Quality:
Beam quality pertains to the ability to focus energy coherently and accurately on a target. Advanced systems like Blue Beam are designed to maintain this coherence over long distances. Contrary to popular belief, the color blue doesn't inherently provide anti-radioactive properties, but certain materials that happen to be blue might offer other forms of protection.

Atmospheric Interference:
Various atmospheric elements can either enhance or diminish a DEW's effectiveness. For example, laser beams can be scattered or absorbed by fog, rain, or humidity. This is a significant factor to consider, especially for airborne DEWs. Imagine a **Cessna** plane equipped with a DEW system; its operational efficacy would vary significantly based on the weather conditions it encounters. If the Cessna is flying at low altitudes where fog is prevalent, the DEW might not be as effective compared to high-altitude, clear-sky scenarios.

Understanding these elements is essential for the development of **DEW**s that can adapt to changing conditions and still deliver their intended effects accurately.

2.5 Power Sources and Storage
The efficacy of a DEW is largely contingent on its power source. This section explores the technologies behind generating and storing the immense energy required for DEWs, from high-energy batteries to compact nuclear reactors and capacitors.

2.6 Targeting and Guidance Systems
For a DEW to be effective, it needs a sophisticated targeting system. With lasers, for example, the speed of engagement is at the speed of light, necessitating real-time or even predictive targeting mechanisms.

2.7 Effects on Targets
Understanding the impact of **DEW**s on their targets is crucial:
Thermal Effects: Numerous DEWs inflict damage by raising the temperature of their targets, resulting in the melting or combustion of materials such as metals and glass. Consider the potential implications for individuals with metallic elements in their bodies, like barium or aluminum. It's crucial to rid the body of these metals. The more metals you get in your body, the higher the chances you exploding.

Electromagnetic Effects: **DEW**s can disrupt, damage, or destroy electronic systems, effectively neutralizing technologically advanced threats without causing structural harm.

Biological Impacts: Some DEWs, especially those designed for crowd control, interact with biological entities, potentially causing discomfort, disorientation, or more severe physiological effects.

2.8 Challenges and Limitations

Despite their potential, DEWs face challenges:

Power and Cooling: Generating and managing high amounts of power, and dealing with the resultant heat, are significant hurdles.

Range and Atmospheric Challenges: Over long distances, atmospheric particles and conditions can reduce a DEW's effectiveness.

Chapter 3:
Historical Development and Milestones of DEWs

3.1 Early Conceptualizations
Even before the development of tangible **DEW** systems, the concept of directing energy as a weapon can be traced back to ancient myths and legends. Perhaps the most famous is Archimedes' supposed "heat ray," where he used mirrors to focus sunlight onto Roman ships, setting them ablaze.
Source: Livio, Mario. *"The Golden Ratio: The Story of Phi, the World's Most Astonishing Number."* Broadway Books, 2003.

3.2 The Birth of Lasers
The laser, a cornerstone of modern DEWs, was born out of the 20th-century scientific revolution. The groundwork was laid by Einstein's quantum theory, but it was only in 1960 that Theodore Maiman created the first functioning ruby laser.
Quote: "A laser is a solution seeking a problem." - Theodore Maiman
Source: Maiman, T.H. *"Stimulated optical radiation in ruby."* Nature 187, 4736 (1960): 493-494.

3.3 Microwave Technology
The development of radar systems during World War II set the stage for understanding and harnessing microwaves, leading to potential DEW applications like the Active Denial System used for crowd control.
Source: Brown, Louis. *"A Radar History of World War II: Technical and Military Imperatives."* CRC Press, 1999.

3.4 Sonic and Ultrasonic Weapons

Sound, though less discussed, offers another avenue for DEWs. Research into sonic and ultrasonic weapons has often been shrouded in secrecy, with potential applications ranging from disorienting adversaries to underwater warfare.

Source: Goodman, Steve. *"Sonic Warfare: Sound, Affect, and the Ecology of Fear."* MIT Press, 2010.

3.5 The Evolution of DEWs: Key Milestones

The progression of Directed Energy Weapons (DEWs) is a testament to the advancements in modern technology and military strategy. From rudimentary concepts to advanced deployment-ready systems, DEWs have traveled an impressive journey.

Early 1970s: The theoretical groundwork for DEWs began, with major defense contractors exploring the potential of lasers and microwaves for military applications.

1980s: Preliminary tests of laser systems by the U.S. military showcased the potential to intercept airborne threats, ushering in considerable investments in DEW research.

Quote: "The 80s weren't just about pop culture; they marked the dawn of a new era in defense technologies." - Dr. Alex Lane, Defense Historian

1990s: Miniaturization and advancements in electronics paved the way for portable DEWs. The focus shifted from bulky systems to more maneuverable and deployable designs.

Early 2000s: DEWs saw their first limited field deployment, mainly for non-lethal crowd control and checkpoint security, demonstrating their utility beyond conventional battlefields.

2015: Lockheed Martin, a leader in defense technologies, made a significant breakthrough, releasing a press statement on their successful test of a 30-kilowatt laser weapon system.
Source: "Lockheed Martin Successfully Tests Advanced Beam Control for Laser Weapons." Lockheed Martin Press Release, March 2015.

2018-2022: The period saw rapid advancements, with major defense players globally showcasing their DEW systems. Operational deployments began, signifying the transition of DEWs from experimental weapons to integrated defense solutions on any targets.

"The pace of DEW development in these years was nothing short of astounding. From concept to combat-ready in just a few decades." - Dr. Alex Lane

2023: With the increasing global tensions, **DEW**s have become pivotal in military strategy, with countries actively integrating these systems into their defense or attack matrix. Recent wildfires, like the purported DEW test in Maui, have pushed the discourse on DEWs to the forefront of international security conversations.

3.6 International Collaborations and Tensions as DEW Race Intensifies

Directed Energy Weapons, with their revolutionary potential, have not only been the focus of intense research and development by individual nations but have also played pivotal roles in international dynamics. These dynamics range from collaborative efforts for shared technological progress to heightened tensions stemming from the power imbalances that such technologies might introduce.

Collaborative Ventures
Several nations, recognizing the shared challenges and potential threats posed by DEWs, have engaged in collaborative research, pooling resources, and expertise to advance this field.
Joint Research Initiatives: Countries within alliances, such as **NATO**, have considered joint research programs to standardize and share advancements in **DEW** technologies. So desesperate.
Shared Defense Systems: Recognizing the global nature of some threats, nations have pondered shared **DEW** defense installations, especially in areas of common interest or where collective defense dynamics play out.

Tensions and Diplomatic Stresses
As with any disruptive technology in the realm of defense, **DEW**s have also been sources of international tensions.
Space Weaponization: **DEW**s have brought the weaponization of space into sharper focus. Despite existing treaties like the Outer Space Treaty, concerns persist about how nations might deploy **DEW**s in orbit, leading to potential arms races in space.
"The weaponization of space not only alters the battlefield but potentially the very ethos of warfare." - Dr. Eleanor N. Williams
Source: Williams, Eleanor N. "Space, the Next Frontier:

Weaponization and Diplomacy." Cambridge Defense Reviews, 2015.

Balance of Power Concerns: The acquisition or advanced development of DEWs by any one nation can cause regional imbalances, prompting neighbors or rivals to accelerate their own DEW programs.
Espionage and Intellectual Property: The race for DEW supremacy has also seen an uptick in espionage cases, with nations trying to gain insights into the DEW progress of their competitors.

Efforts at DEW Control and Limitation
Realizing the destabilizing potential of unchecked DEW development and deployment, international bodies and diplomatic forums have taken initial steps to discuss potential arms control or limitation agreements concerning DEWs.

Global Forums: The United Nations, in particular, has held preliminary discussions about the implications of DEWs for global peace and security.

Regional Dialogues: Regional organizations have also taken up the DEW dialogue, understanding that localized imbalances can lead to broader conflicts.

The evolving landscape of DEWs on the international stage underscores their transformative potential, not just for warfare, but for diplomacy, collaboration, and potential conflict. As nations grapple with the implications of this technology, the world watches, hoping that collective wisdom prevails over individual ambitions.

3.7 Current Leaders in DEW Research

The Landscape of Directed Energy Weapons (DEWs)
The 21st century has seen a seismic shift in the manner of warfare. As technology has advanced, nations have sought to harness its power for military purposes. Directed Energy Weapons (DEWs) have emerged at the forefront of this revolution. Several countries, realizing the game-changing potential of these weapons, have plunged into deep research and development.

"In the realm of warfare, DEWs are not just a shift; they represent an evolution. Their silent operation, precise targeting, and instantaneous impact challenge the very fabric of traditional defense mechanisms." - Dr. Angela Robertson, Defense Technologist
Source: Robertson, Angela. "The Silent Evolution: DEWs in Modern Warfare." Defense Technology Analysis, 2021.

United States: A Forerunner in Innovation
The US, with its immense defense budget and technological prowess, has taken a lead role. Agencies like **DARPA** and giants like Lockheed Martin and Raytheon have made significant strides.
Speed and Precision: The *US Navy's Laser Weapon System* (LaWS) is a testament to rapid targeting and high accuracy. Deployed on ships, it offers a defense against drones and other threats.
Interview Insights: Rear Admiral Brian Luther, in an interview with Defense News, mentioned, *"LaWS isn't just about shooting down threats; it's about redefining how we engage in naval warfare."*
Website Reference: US Navy Official Page on LaWS

Russia: Merging Tradition with Futurism
Russia, while traditionally focusing on conventional warfare, has realized the DEW potential, gradually integrating this tech into their defense strategies.

Technology Focus: Their **Peresvet** combat laser system, officially entered into service, is believed to offer a range of defense capabilities. <u>**All four planes used by the Russian president have countermeasures against Direct Energy Weapons**</u> (DEW).
"Russia's interest in DEWs signifies a merging of its traditional show of strength with cutting-edge technology." - **Prof. Ivan Kuznetsov,** Moscow State University
Source: Kuznetsov, Ivan. "Russia's Dance with Directed Energy." Moscow Military Review, 2021.

China: Emerging Powerhouse in DEW Tech
China's rise as a global superpower extends to the domain of DEWs, where their advancements, often shrouded in secrecy, suggest a rapidly developing capability.
Tech Display: Defense exhibitions in Beijing have showcased <u>laser systems</u> designed to intercept and neutralize threats, pointing to China's growing prowess.
Interview Insights: A conversation with Dr. Li Wei, a defense analyst, in the South China Morning Post highlighted that *"China views DEWs as an integral part of its future defense. The progress might be silent but is swift."*
Website Reference: South China Morning Post Defense Section

Israel: Pioneering Tactical Integration
Israel, with its unique security challenges, has always been at the cutting edge of defense technologies. DEWs are no exception.

Operational Use: The Iron Beam, a laser air-defense system, aims to complement the famed Iron Dome, targeting short-range threats with <u>remarkable precision.</u>
"For Israel, every advancement in defense, including DEWs, is not just strategy; it's survival." - Col. Yitzhak Tzur, Israeli Defense Forces
Source: Tzur, Yitzhak. "Israel's Laser Focus: DEWs in Tactical Defense." Jerusalem Defense Review, 2020.

Chapter 4: Modern Applications and Implications of DEWs
4.1 Defense and Strategic Uses
While DEWs have a plethora of potential applications, their most prominent and debated use is in the defense sector. Modern militaries are exploring DEWs not only <u>for offense but also for defense</u> against incoming threats like missiles and drones.
Source: Smith, Lorraine. "Directed Energy: The Evolution of War." Defense Today, 2021.

4.2 Civilian and Law Enforcement Applications

Bridging the Lethality Gap
The utilization of Directed Energy Weapons (DEWs) is not restricted to the world of military combat. In civil arenas, the concept of using force effectively without resulting in permanent harm or fatality is of utmost importance. DEWs, in this aspect, provide a potentially transformative solution.
"Directed energy offers a non-lethal alternative, bridging the gap between passive restraint and lethal force." - **Chief Adrian Rodriguez**

Source: Rodriguez, Adrian. "Modern Policing: The Role of Non-lethal Technologies." Law Enforcement Journal, 2020.

Crowd Control: A Shift from Physical to Directed Force

For law enforcement agencies worldwide, managing large crowds, especially during protests or riots, is a challenging task. Traditional methods such as water cannons, tear gas, or rubber bullets can lead to unintentional injuries.

Active Denial Systems (ADS): <u>Developed initially for military applications, ADS emits a directed beam of microwave energy that produces a burning sensation on the skin, causing targeted individuals to reflexively move away</u>. This **"pain ray"** offers a way to disperse crowds without direct physical confrontation.

Source: Thompson, Gary. "The Future of Crowd Control: ADS and its Implications." Public Safety Magazine, 2019.

Perimeter Defense: Keeping Intruders at Bay

Protecting vital infrastructure, such as power plants, research facilities, and governmental buildings, petrol stations requires layered defense mechanisms. DEWs offer an additional layer, acting as a deterrent for potential intruders.

Laser Deterrent Systems: Some facilities have begun testing laser systems that can temporarily blind or disorient intruders, preventing them from progressing further into a protected area.
Source: Malik, Sarah. "Laser Defense: A New Era of Perimeter Security." Security Innovations Monthly, 2021.

Wildlife Deterrence: A Novel Application

Airports globally face a constant challenge: wildlife, especially birds, that pose a risk to aircraft during takeoffs and landings.

Traditional methods, like loud noises or physical barriers, have had mixed results.
Optical Deterrence: By using non-harmful laser systems, airports can create "light barriers". Birds and other animals perceive these as physical obstructions, effectively deterring them from entering runway areas.
"It's a dance of light and instinct. Birds see the DEW barriers as tangible threats, ensuring our skies remain safer." - Dr. Amelia Clarkson, Avian Behavior Specialist
Source: Clarkson, Amelia. "Dancing with Light: DEWs in Wildlife Management." Airport Safety Quarterly, 2022.

The integration of **Directed Energy Weapons** in civilian and law enforcement scenarios showcases their versatility and potential for non-lethal applications or beyond... While ethical and practical considerations remain, the promise of more controlled, effective, and safer means of applying force in various non-combat situations is undeniably appealing. As technology advances, the refinement of DEWs for such applications will be a space to watch closely.

4.3 Space Applications
With space becoming an arena for geopolitics, DEWs are being looked at both as a means of defense against hostile satellites and as a potential tool for satellite maintenance by removing space debris...
Source: Johnston, Alice. "Space Defense: The Directed Energy Frontier." Orbital Review, 2022.

4.4 Technological Disruption and Countermeasures
As with all technologies, DEWs can be both a boon and a bane. There's a growing concern about their potential misuse, leading to an arms race of sorts in developing countermeasures.
Source: Patel, Rajesh. "Energy in Equilibrium: Countering the DEW Threat." *Global Defense Review*, 2023.

4.5 Environmental Implications
The deployment of DEWs, especially on a large scale, could have environmental implications. While they promise cleaner engagements than traditional munitions, there are concerns about their long-term impact on ecosystems.

Source: Green, Henry. "Directed Energy: An Environmental Perspective." *Ecological Watch*, 2021.

4.6 Ethical and Legal Debates
The emergence of **Directed Energy Weapons** (DEWs) has raised unprecedented ethical and legal concerns, particularly in terms of their covert nature, the potential lack of physical evidence, and the challenges they present in determining accountability.

Identifying the Victim and Mourning
One of the most profound challenges posed by <u>DEWs is the absence of a physical body in cases of fatality</u>. This absence can be deeply troubling for families and communities. Mourning rituals across cultures often involve the body as a central element, serving as a conduit for closure and remembrance. The process of grieving, a deeply human experience, might become an emotional labyrinth when there's no tangible proof of a loved one's demise. The existential question arises: **how does**

one mourn for someone when there's no body to mourn over?
Moreover, the physical absence complicates the process of post-mortem investigations, making it difficult to establish the cause of death. It challenges the forensic norms and demands the development of advanced methodologies to ascertain DEW-related fatalities.

Establishing Proof and Legal Challenges
The very nature of DEWs, where the evidence of an attack may be minimal or non-existent, poses daunting challenges for the legal system. When traditional forensic evidence such as wounds or projectiles is absent, how does one prove an attack? This uncertainty might lead to a lack of accountability and justice, as victims or their families could struggle to provide evidence in courts.

Additionally, the ambiguity surrounding DEW attacks could provoke false claims. With the increasing awareness of these weapons, there's a potential risk of attributing unexplained incidents to DEW strikes without concrete evidence.

Truth-seeking and Transparency
In the era of DEWs, the quest for the truth becomes more intricate. Governments or organizations with the capability to deploy such weapons might do so covertly, leading to a shroud of secrecy and misinformation. How do nations ensure transparency in their defense operations? How do global communities establish checks and balances for countries wielding these tools?

International Law and Warfare Ethics
As quoted by Professor **Malena Olsson**, the stealth nature of DEWs challenges the core tenets of warfare ethics and

international law. The principles of distinction (differentiating between combatants and civilians) and proportionality (ensuring that harm caused during an attack is proportional to the military advantage) are foundational to **the laws of war.** DEWs, with their precision and potential for clandestine use, can blur these lines, making it crucial for international bodies to reassess and redefine existing conventions.

Furthermore, the covert use of DEWs might bypass the formal declarations of war or conflict, pushing engagements into the shadows, away from international scrutiny and potential diplomatic resolutions.

The advent of Directed Energy Weapons has ushered in a new era of warfare and defense strategies, bringing along a host of ethical and legal conundrums. As technology continues to advance, it is imperative for international communities, legal scholars, ethicists, and policymakers to collaborate, ensuring that the evolution of warfare tools doesn't outpace our moral and legal frameworks. The collective endeavor should aim at safeguarding human rights, ensuring accountability, and promoting transparency in this new landscape of defense technology.

4.7 Economic Impact

The research, development, and deployment of DEWs have broad economic ramifications. As nations invest in this technology, there's potential for job creation, innovation, and the emergence of ancillary industries, but for which purposes?.

Source: Lim, Frederick. *"Economic Horizons: The Rise of Directed Energy Markets." Financial Times Annual, 2023.*

In Chapter 4, we delve deeper into the multifaceted applications of DEWs, extending beyond the realms of military and defense.

The implications of these technologies span various sectors, and understanding them is crucial for policymakers, researchers, and the general public alike.

Chapter 5: DEWs in the Global Landscape
5.1 Global Proliferation and DEW Development
With technological advancements, more countries are gaining access to DEW technology. This section will explore the global proliferation of DEWs, highlighting key nations and their respective advancements.
Source: Anderson, Karen. "Directed Energy Proliferation: A Global Snapshot." International Defense Journal, 2022.

5.2 The Diplomacy of DEWs
As with all potent weapons, the deployment and usage of DEWs have diplomatic implications. Understanding how nations navigate these challenges is critical for predicting geopolitical shifts.
Quote: "DEWs are not just tools of warfare; they are tools of diplomacy, reshaping the very fabric of international relations." - Ambassador John L. Matthews
Source: Matthews, John L. "Diplomacy in the Age of Directed Energy." Foreign Affairs Quarterly, 2023.

5.3 Potential Flashpoints and Geopolitical Implications
Certain global regions are more susceptible to tensions stemming from DEW developments. Identifying these flashpoints can provide insights into future conflict zones.
Source: Zhao, Liang. "Hotspots in the Age of DEWs." Asian Defense Review, 2022.

5.4 DEWs and the New Arms Race
Drawing parallels to the Cold War-era nuclear arms race, there are growing concerns about a new arms race centered on DEWs. This section dives into this evolving dynamic.
Source: Fitzgerald, Michael. "The Next Arms Race: Lasers, Microwaves, and Global Tensions." Modern War Studies, 2021.

5.5 International Treaties and Regulatory Challenges
Given their potential for covert use and immense destructive capability, international treaties and regulations on DEWs are paramount. Here, we'll explore existing agreements and the pressing need for new ones.
Source: Kumar, Priya. "Directed Energy and International Law: Navigating the Uncharted." International Law Review, 2023.

5.6 Collaborative Research and Shared Concerns
Not all aspects of DEWs on the global stage are confrontational. Many nations are realizing the mutual benefits of collaborative research, especially in areas like countermeasures and environmental impacts.
Source: Ngo, Binh. "Harnessing Energy Together: Global Collaborations in DEW Research." Global Science Journal, 2021.

5.7 The Role of Non-State Actors
As DEWs become more accessible and portable, the likelihood of them falling into the hands of non-state actors, including terrorist organizations and private corporations, grows alarmingly. This raises pressing questions about how we can distinguish between legitimate use and misuse, particularly in complex scenarios.

Example: The Cessna 560 Citation Dilemma

Imagine a situation where a terrorist organization acquires a Cessna 560 Citation, <u>a common business jet</u>. Now consider that this aircraft is retrofitted with DEWs. Flying alongside other business jets that are often seen as innocuous, this weaponized Cessna would present a formidable challenge for security agencies. From the outside, the terrorist-operated plane would look virtually identical to any other Cessna 560 Citation in the sky, making it nearly impossible to distinguish between a harmless civilian aircraft and a devastating weapon of terror.

Such a situation would call for extraordinary measures, likely involving extensive background checks on aircraft ownership, increased scrutiny of flight paths, and perhaps even the deployment of counter-DEW technologies in strategic locations.

But these measures would themselves raise ethical and logistical questions about privacy, profiling, and the freedom of the skies.

As Dr. Aisha Al-Rahman points out, *the lines are increasingly blurring between state and non-state actors in the age of DEWs. This challenges our existing security paradigms and forces us to rethink strategies to protect civilian life without infringing on individual liberties.* Is everybody seeing what I see ?

Implications for Security Policies
The possibility of non-state actors acquiring DEWs calls for a multi-pronged approach that includes tightening export controls, enhancing surveillance capabilities, and fostering international cooperation to monitor the acquisition and use of such technologies.

While we may enact stringent laws and develop advanced technologies to counter these threats, the emergence of DEWs in the hands of non-state actors represents an evolving challenge that will require persistent vigilance and adaptive strategies.
Source: Al-Rahman, Aisha. "Non-State Actors in the DEW Era." Security and Strategy Quarterly, 2022.

Chapter 6: Looking Ahead - DEWs in the Future and the Maui Event of August 2023

6.1 The Technological Evolution of DEWs
As with all technologies, DEWs will continue to evolve. This section delves into the potential pathways of their progression, including miniaturization, increased power outputs, and integration with other technologies.
Source: Walters, Julian. "The Next Generation of DEWs." Futuristic Defense, 2023.

6.2 Economic and Industrial Growth
With the rise of DEWs, industries related to their production, maintenance, and deployment will flourish. Here, we'll explore the potential economic boons and sectors poised for growth.
Source: Harrington, Luke. "Economic Frontiers: DEW Industries." Global Economic Review, 2023.

6.3 The Maui Event of August 2023
In a significant demonstration of DEW capability, the probable Maui event served as a turning point in public perception and understanding of Directed Energy Weapons to accelerate Smart cities projects. We dissect the event, its outcomes, and its implications. I'm simply asking questions like…
Why does the fire burn in rings in Maui like a perfect circle ?
Do you see the same thing that I see?

The same similarities to places like Paradise California ?
The paradise is the target everywhere ?

Do you think it odds that they turned away help?

Do you think it odds they felt to warn resident ?

Do you find it odd that emergency alert sirens did not go off, more than 80 sirens on Maui , 400 for ALL Hawai?

Do you think it's normal the palm trees did not burnt ?

Even the boat in the sea were burning, why ?

That deserves answers for. Question everything...

From the outset of the Maui wildfires, it's a mix of a perfect storm and sheer incompetence. However, there are two aspects that cannot be overlooked. Everyone has seen the photographs of cars double-parked on Front Street in Lahaina, where people had to abandon their vehicles and jump into the ocean to flee the flames:
All the glass is gone.
The melting point of glass is 2,600 degrees. A wildfire reaches 1,500 degrees. That's a 1,100-degree difference in temperature.

Not a single piece of glass remains on these vehicles. Except... a blue car... (see chapter 7.1.1 for more explanation)

How can that be?

Another observation: <u>not a single car door is open</u>. If these individuals were trapped by fire and had to leap from their vehicles to escape the flames, wouldn't there be an open car door here or there?

Did every person who jumped out of those cars actually close their door before diving into the ocean?

Was this truly a "natural" disaster?

Nature has certainly shifted, if that were the case. They kept the public in the dark... Wear blue shirts. This event isn't an anomaly., it's more The same types of wildfires are now being witnessed in Texas, Washington, and Oregon. Something seems off...

Even the Simpsons, in their typical prescient fashion, alluded to it in their "*We Will Rebuild*" episode. To be in a protective bubble, like in Simpson buy a blue car, wear a blue shirt, and paint your houses in blue. IN the Simpson episode the status is covered with a blue turps. It's the only thing survive. Not enough weird ?

Additionally, Mountain Dew, the well-known brand, introduced a beverage named **Maui Blast** with a pineapple flavor. Does that clarify things? Do you read between the lines? Wake up!

However, amidst the chaos, insurance companies have opted NOT to fund reconstruction, citing that residents didn't "comply" with the new city code.

How can a fire spread so rapidly in 74% humidity?

Smart meters in homes could be both the cause and the explanation. They are equipped with lithium batteries. When ignited, they burn uncontrollably, much like a burning electric vehicle. There was a distinct haze in the air over Maui...

What happened in Hawai ?

They claim it's due to climate change... Really? Who's manipulating the climate? Perhaps watch the movie, "*The Light Bulb Conspiracy.*" Under a blue umbrella.
Mountain **Dew**, the brand, released a drink called **Maui Blast**, pineapple-flavored. Is this predictive programming? Everything is written.

"Maui wasn't just a test; it was a proclamation to the world of a new era in warfare and defense." - General Robert K. Lyons
Source: Thompson, Patricia News "Maui News 2023: The DEW Demonstration that Shook the World." Defense Digest, Special Edition Summer 2023

6.4 Military and DEWs

Beyond their applications in military and defense, the emergence of DEWs will undeniably influence society at large, as evidenced by the event this past August. Surveillance Awareness Technology or Directed Energy, a division of the US Military stationed at *Kirkland Air Force Base*, which is now a part of the US Space Force, is located in… **Maui.** This one is called The Air Force Maui Optimal and Supercomputing Site (AMOS), the other one is in New Mexico. One of the mission is laser propagation through the Earth atmosphere as stated in AFRIl doc, in Directte Energy Directorate .

Source: Martinez, Isabella. "Society in the Age of Directed Energy." And Military Web Site Social Futures Journal, 2023 and AFRI (The Air Force Research Laboratory

6.5 Environmental and Space Considerations

The advent and potential deployment of DEWs, both on Earth's surface and beyond, present multifaceted environmental challenges and considerations:

Atmospheric Impact: The use of DEWs can cause localized atmospheric heating, potentially leading to meteorological disturbances. For instance, high-energy lasers can create temporary high-pressure zones which can influence weather patterns in the immediate vicinity.
"The potential for DEWs to affect local weather systems, even inadvertently, is a growing concern among environmentalists." - Dr. Rebecca Farrow, Atmospheric Scientist

Ozone Layer Interaction: There is potential for certain DEW frequencies to interact with the ozone layer, which could lead to its depletion if used intensively and frequently.

Space Debris: If DEWs are used in space warfare or defense, they might result in the creation of additional space debris. Such debris can pose risks to other satellites, the International Space Station, and future space missions.
"With every satellite or object we destroy in space using DEWs, we risk creating thousands of new projectiles in an already cluttered environment." - Astronomer Dr. Miles O'Brien

Space Ecosystems: The notion of a "space ecosystem" is still in its infancy. However, there's concern about how DEWs might interact with the microgravity environment, potentially affecting studies and experiments in space.

Haze Phenomenon: The use of DEWs can produce haze or smog-like conditions due to the rapid heating and

subsequent cooling of the air. This can reduce visibility and may have implications for both ground and aerial activities in the affected region. In places like Maui, the observed haze by the locals could be a byproduct of DEWs or other related activities, although more research is needed to confirm such hypotheses.
Source: Wagner, Leo. *"Directed Energy Weapons and Atmospheric Implications."* Environmental Science Journal, 2022 and TT.

Flora and Fauna Impact: There's potential for DEWs to affect both plant and animal life, especially if used in terrestrial settings. The rapid heating can affect plant health, while certain frequencies might be harmful to wildlife, especially those sensitive to electromagnetic fields.
In summary, while DEWs promise new frontiers in defense and technology, they also pose unique environmental challenges. As with any emerging technology, the implications - both positive and negative - must be thoroughly understood and addressed in their deployment and usage for the best or the worst.

6.6 Strategies for Global Cooperation
As nations grapple with the challenges and opportunities of DEWs, there's a pressing need for global cooperation. This section proposes frameworks and strategies for collaborative efforts.
Source: Okonjo, Nneka. *"Bridging Divides: A Blueprint for Global Cooperation on DEWs."* International Peace & Diplomacy Journal, 2023.

6.7 Envisioning the 2030 Landscape
Taking a speculative yet informed approach, this section paints a picture of the world in 2030, influenced heavily by the integration of DEWs in various sectors.
Source: Lee, Harrison. *"2030: A DEW-Driven World."* Future Projections Magazine, 2023.

Chapter 7: Countermeasures and Defense Against DEWs

7.1 Understanding the DEW Threat Spectrum

Directed Energy Weapons (DEWs) operate over a broad range of the electromagnetic spectrum. This vastness presents both opportunities for novel applications and challenges for defense mechanisms. Each portion of the spectrum, from radio waves to visible light and beyond, carries its unique set of characteristics that influence how **DEW**s can be employed and how they can be countered. One particular area of interest lies in understanding why certain colors or frequencies, notably those in the blue range, might have resistance or unique interactions with DEWs.

Source: Mitchell, Donna. "The DEW Spectrum: From Lasers to Microwaves." Defense Tech Review Newsletter, 2022.

7.1.1 High-Powered Lasers (HPLs) and the Mystery of the Blue Spectrum

High-Powered Lasers (HPLs) represent one of the most well-known types of DEWs. They operate by focusing an intense beam of light onto a target, leading to immediate and precise damage. However, not all light is created equal when it comes to laser operation. **The energy and behavior of a laser are highly dependent on its wavelength**. While HPLs can operate across the visible spectrum and beyond, recent studies have indicated that lasers might exhibit <u>diminished effects when interacting with blue-colored materials.</u>

<u>**The blue part of the spectrum has shorter wavelengths and higher frequencies compared to the**</u>

45

red end. This characteristic means that blue light carries more energy per photon. <u>As such, materials or coatings that reflect or absorb in the blue spectrum might exhibit a natural resilience against certain DEWs</u>, effectively dispersing or reflecting the energy rather than absorbing it.

Furthermore, some theoretical and applied research has pointed out that certain materials, when engineered to have properties that interact favorably with the blue end of the spectrum, can act as effective countermeasures against HPLs. These materials can either diffuse the energy of the laser or create interference patterns that reduce the laser's potency.

Another aspect to consider is the atmosphere. <u>Blue light scatters more in the atmosphere due to Rayleigh scattering, the same reason the sky appears blue</u>. Therefore, DEWs operating in the blue spectrum might face challenges related to range and atmospheric interference, this explains why building in blue will resist better.
However, it's essential to understand that these findings do not render HPLs ineffective. <u>They simply present a potential vulnerability that can be exploited for defense</u>, and equally, strategies can be developed to overcome these limitations in offensive capacities. *Source: Wagner, Gerald & Mc Thomson, Ralf. "Blue's Resistance: The Interaction of HPLs with the Blue Spectrum." Journal of Laser Defense Studies Newsletter, 2022*

Let's explore these aspects in-depth. Blue is Everything.

There are properties of blue light and materials that predominantly reflect or emit <u>blue light which can influence how they interact with DEWs</u>.

Rayleigh Scattering: Blue light scatters more readily in the atmosphere due to its shorter wavelength, a phenomenon known as **Rayleigh scattering**. This is why the sky appears blue. If a DEW operates in or around the **blue spectrum**, its energy can scatter more, making it potentially less effective over long distances. If a target is blue because it scatters blue light (rather than absorbing it), then it could scatter some portion of the DEW's energy, making the DEW slightly less effective.

But let's delve deeper: why have foreigners colored their roofs blue for their mansions? As we know, blue is everything, and everything is connected. These blue umbrellas, untouched by the wildfire in **Maui,** along with blue boats, blue cars, and blue shirts, all survived the wildfires. The clue could be that, in the law of the universe, the recipient of your actions must be aware of your actions to avoid receiving bad karma. So, if you want to do something bad, you might put it in cartoon movies, like the *Simpsons*. The blue shirts found belong to the company *Sister Revolution*, based in **Baja** California, similar to the Mountain Dew **Baja** Blast. Why does blue survive wildfires or attacks?

Absorption and Reflection:

Materials that appear blue do so because they absorb other wavelengths and reflect blue wavelengths. **If a material strongly reflects blue light, it might also reflect other nearby wavelengths, potentially making it more resistant to DEWs operating in those wavelengths**. However, this is a function of the material's specific reflective properties, not the color blue only...

Spectral Absorption Windows: Every material has specific absorption and transmission windows across different wavelengths. If a material is transparent to the specific wavelength of a DEW, it won't absorb much of its energy, and vice versa. If a target material (that happens to be blue) has an absorption window that doesn't align with the DEW's frequency, then it would be less affected by that DEW.

Thermal Properties: If we hypothesize that a blue material reflects more energy, it could potentially heat up less when exposed to DEWs, depending on the DEW's operating spectrum. This would be relevant if the DEW works by heating the target. The thermal conductivity and heat capacity of the material would also play a significant role in determining its vulnerability.

Non-Linear Optical Properties: Some materials, when exposed to intense light of a certain frequency, can exhibit non-linear effects like frequency doubling. If a blue material had such properties, it might alter the incoming DEW beam in unpredictable ways.

Thus, while there can be specific scenarios or materials where the color or properties associated with blue might provide some level of resistance to DEWs, <u>it's not accurate to make a blanket statement that "blue cannot be attacked by DEW or less."</u> The actual interaction would depend on the material's properties also.

7.1.2 Microwave Emitters

Microwave emitters operate within the frequency range of roughly 300 MHz to 400 GHz. They deliver focused bursts of energy at specific frequencies to interfere with electronics. For instance, **a microwave emitter targeting a communication device might operate around 2.4 GHz, the common frequency for Wi-Fi.** Alternatively, if targeting a radar system, the emitter might be tuned to its specific operating frequency, e.g., 10 GHz for certain radar bands.

Challenges:
Their broad frequency spectrum can inadvertently affect both friendly and adversarial systems. A blast intended to disable enemy comms might also disrupt allied systems operating on similar frequencies.

Microwave emissions, especially when used in a broad-spectrum manner, can make it challenging to identify the source, providing attackers a degree of anonymity.

In an age where modern warfare leans heavily on electronic systems for communication, surveillance, and control, microwave emitters pose a particularly grave threat. Countermeasures, like Faraday cages or frequency hopping, become essential for defense.

7.1.3 Radio Frequency (RF) Weapons

Radio Frequency (RF) weapons specifically target the wide spectrum of frequencies used in wireless communication, which spans from roughly 3 kHz to 300 GHz. These devices are designed to overwhelm or "jam" communication channels, leading to interference or total signal loss. For instance, on a battlefield, if an infantry unit relies on a 400 MHz frequency for their radios, an RF weapon can flood that frequency, rendering communication tools useless.

While RF weapons do not usually inflict direct physical damage, their capacity to sever communication lines can be a pivotal tactical advantage. A unit that cannot communicate becomes strategically blind and is more susceptible to misinformation, mis-coordination, or ambush. Furthermore, with modern warfare and global businesses heavily leaning on satellite communications, which typically operate in the L-band (1 to 2 GHz) or Ku-band (12 to 18 GHz), the interruption of these channels can have reverberating consequences, affecting everything from military operations to global commerce.

Challenges:
The disruption of communication does more than just silence a unit. It creates chaos, mistrust, and confusion. A team unable to relay or receive information may inadvertently venture into hostile territories or fail to execute synchronized maneuvers.
The world's increasing reliance on satellite communication magnifies the risk posed by RF weapons. A successful attack on satellite channels can cascade into a multifaceted crisis, crippling military, financial, and civilian communication systems. In a hyper-connected age, the cascading effects of such a disruption can be both immediate and far-reaching.

7.1.4 Particle Beams

Particle beams represent the next frontier in Directed Energy Weaponry, working on the principle of accelerating charged or neutral particles to high velocities. Conceptually, it's akin to using a focused stream of atomic or subatomic particles as a **"bullet"** – an idea inspired by our understanding of particle accelerators in physics labs. When these particles collide with a target, they can release their kinetic energy, resulting in immense heat and potentially catastrophic damage.

Blue beams, for instance, might be conceptualized as a type of particle beam that leverages a specific spectrum of energy, perhaps resonating or being more efficient within **the blue spectrum**. This specificity might lend advantages like improved targeting or reduced atmospheric interference, given the unique properties of blue light wavelengths which are around 450-495 nm.

Challenges:
The sheer amount of energy needed to propel particles at destructive speeds is immense, making the logistics of power generation and storage a significant hurdle.

Shielding equipment from the intense radiation and electromagnetic fields generated by these beams poses a unique challenge. Materials and design concepts that can withstand these forces and protect operators are still in development.

Given the largely theoretical nature of particle beams, devising strategies and technologies to counteract or defend against them remains in its infancy. We have yet to see practical, tested defenses against such sophisticated technology.

7.1.5 Acoustic Weapons

Acoustic weapons have surfaced as an intriguing subset of DEWs, employing sound waves that span different frequency ranges. While we often associate sound with what we hear, these weapons harness both the inaudible infrasound (below 20 Hz) and ultrasound (above 20 kHz) spectrums. The impact can range from subtle psychological disturbances with infrasound to potential tissue damage with high-powered ultrasound. For instance, at certain frequencies and intensity levels, these waves can resonate with human organs or even disrupt electronic components.

Challenges:
Most conventional protective gear, designed with kinetic threats in mind, offers limited protection against focused acoustic energy. This means that even in full combat gear, troops could be vulnerable to these non-traditional attacks.
The nature of sound makes it inherently challenging to determine its origin. Unlike a bullet's trajectory or a missile's flight path, sound can refract and reflect off surfaces, making source determination a daunting task.

The effectiveness of acoustic weapons is inherently variable. Depending on factors such as distance, environmental conditions, and the specific frequency used, results can range from mild discomfort to severe physical consequences. Adjusting for these variables in real-time battlefield conditions remains a challenge.

7.2 Traditional Defense Mechanisms

The introduction of DEWs into modern warfare and security scenarios challenges our established understanding of defense. Traditional mechanisms, which have stood the test of time against kinetic weaponry, are now under scrutiny for their efficacy against energy-based threats.
Source: Kim, Soo-Jin. "Old Meets New: Conventional Defenses in the DEW Age." *Military Innovation Journal,* 2023.

7.2.1 Armor and Physical Barriers
The time-tested reliance on armor, ranging from fortified structures to vehicle armor, has primarily been to deflect or absorb kinetic damage. But how does metal or concrete fare against high-powered lasers or microwaves?
Challenges:
Conventional materials can act as conductors for energy-based attacks, potentially spreading damage.
Over-reliance on thickness can lead to increased weight and decreased mobility.

7.2.2 Electro-Magnetic Shielding

Electro-magnetic shielding, traditionally employed to safeguard against electronic eavesdropping or secure critical equipment from electromagnetic interference (EMI), presents itself as a potential line of defense against the threat of DEWs. At its core, this shielding operates by creating a barrier, often using materials like conductive or magnetic compounds, which reflects or absorbs the electromagnetic radiation. This means it can, theoretically, deflect or reduce the energy of DEWs, especially those that operate within certain electromagnetic spectrums.

Challenges:
The effectiveness of electromagnetic shielding is not universally consistent across all DEW types. For instance, a shield that effectively protects against a high-frequency laser might be less efficacious against a microwave emitter. The broad spectrum of DEWs demands a versatile shielding solution, which currently remains a technological challenge.

As we move towards more mobile warfare units, integrating electromagnetic shielding on infantry or agile aircraft becomes a significant obstacle. Not only do the materials add weight, but they may also interfere with the unit's own electronic systems or reduce maneuverability. Balancing protection with practicality is a nuanced task that demands innovative engineering solutions.

Furthermore, as DEWs evolve and diversify, so too must shielding. Predicting and countering the ever-advancing technology of DEWs is like a high-tech game of cat and mouse, with each side striving to outdo the other in capabilities and countermeasures. This dynamism calls for continual research, adaptation, and investment in electromagnetic protection methodologies.

7.2.3 Camouflage and Stealth
DEWs require precise targeting. Camouflage, historically used to blend into surroundings, and modern stealth technologies,

designed to deflect or absorb radar, might provide some advantages.

Challenges:

DEWs using non-visual targeting methods can still locate camouflaged or stealthy units.

Maintenance and cost of stealth technologies are high.

7.3 The Role of Materials Science

7.2.3 Camouflage and Stealth

Camouflage and stealth technologies have long been part of the defense industry's toolkit. In the age of Directed Energy Weapons (DEWs), they offer a two-fold defense strategy that is increasingly complicated but potentially effective.

Example 1: Adaptive Camouflage

Imagine a vehicle or a unit equipped with adaptive camouflage that can mimic the surrounding environment in real-time. This could be highly effective against laser-based DEWs that rely on optical targeting. However, it presents challenges because DEWs utilizing infrared or other non-visual means of targeting could still pinpoint the location of the camouflaged unit. Plus, adaptive camouflage technology can be expensive to develop and maintain, making it less feasible for widespread use.

Example 2: Radar-Absorbing Stealth Coatings

Another approach could be the use of advanced stealth coatings designed to absorb radar waves, making the object virtually 'invisible' to radar-based **DEW**s. Military aircraft like the *F-35 Lightning II* use similar stealth technologies. Yet, even this sophisticated solution is not foolproof. For instance, it requires ongoing maintenance, including frequent reapplication of the coatings, which increases the logistical and financial burden.

Moreover, as DEW technology advances, we could see the development of targeting systems that can overcome such stealth features.

Challenges:

Non-Visual Targeting: Modern DEWs often use non-visual targeting methods like infrared or radar, making even the most advanced camouflage and stealth technologies vulnerable.

High Maintenance and Costs: The technologies required to make units stealthy or camouflaged are intricate and expensive. They often require regular updates and maintenance, adding to the overall cost of the defense system.

Counter-Advancements: As DEWs evolve, so do their targeting capabilities. Today's stealth technology may be obsolete tomorrow, requiring continual adaptation and innovation to remain effective.

Given these challenges, while camouflage and stealth can offer some advantages in the DEW landscape, they are not standalone solutions. They should be part of a broader, more integrated defense strategy that also considers other forms of protection and deterrence.

7.3.1 Reflective Surfaces : the mirror

Reflective surfaces stand as a potentially potent countermeasure against laser-based DEWs. The logic is straightforward: if a laser's energy can be reflected instead of being absorbed by the target, it reduces the potential harm. However, the challenge isn't just about reflecting light, but about reflecting the specific frequencies and intensities that DEWs can employ.

Advancements:

Development of Meta-materials: Beyond traditional reflective materials, the advent of meta-materials has revolutionized this defense. Meta-materials are artificially structured materials used to control and manipulate light. For instance, scientists have been working on materials that can reflect or refract specific laser wavelengths, making them ideal for countering specific types of laser DEWs. A good example of this would be the creation of materials that can bend light around an object, rendering it invisible or significantly reducing the impact of the laser.

Mirror Technology: At its most basic, **a mirror can indeed be an effective tool against some laser DEWs**, especially if the mirror has a high-quality, highly-reflective surface. The challenge lies in keeping the mirror's surface pristine, as even minor imperfections or debris can diminish its reflective capabilities. Moreover, a mirror might reflect the laser back to its source or towards another unintended target, leading to collateral damage.

Integration into Protective Gear and Vehicles: As meta-materials evolve, we see attempts to integrate them into military assets. Imagine tanks with surfaces designed to reflect DEWs or soldiers wearing armor that refracts laser energy away from vital organs. Research is ongoing in this area, with prototypes being tested for their efficacy in real-world scenarios.

However, it's worth noting that no defense is absolute. While reflective surfaces can provide a robust shield against laser DEWs, they need to be coupled with other protective measures to ensure comprehensive defense against the broader spectrum of DEW threats.

7.3.2 Absorbent Compounds
Rather than reflecting energy, some materials are being designed to absorb and dissipate it, thereby reducing the direct damage.
Advancements:
High-entropy alloys known for their heat resistance and dissipation capabilities.
Nano-structured materials that trap and scatter directed energy at a microscopic level.

7.3.3 Adaptive and Responsive Materials
The next frontier is materials that can adapt in real-time to the threats they face, changing their properties to offer the best defense against a specific DEW type.
Advancements:
Polymers that change structure in response to heat or electromagnetic fields.
Surfaces embedded with sensors that can detect incoming DEW threats and activate countermeasures.

7.3 The Role of Materials Science
In the age of DEWs, materials science plays a pivotal role. From reflective surfaces to absorbent compounds, this segment delves into the forefront of research on materials designed to mitigate the effects of directed energy.
Quote: "The key to defending against DEWs may not be in electronics, but in the very fabric and materials we develop." - Dr. Carlos Alvarez, Materials Scientist
Source: Alvarez, Carlos. "Material Innovations Against Directed Energy." Advanced Materials Digest, 2022.

7.4 Electronic and Cyber Countermeasures

7.4 Electronic and Cyber Countermeasures

Directed Energy Weapons (DEWs) are not stand-alone systems; they are a part of a complex web of electronic architecture that makes them both potent and vulnerable. As DEWs are digital-first technologies, leveraging electronics for targeting, triggering, and firing, they are susceptible to a variety of electronic countermeasures.

7.4.1 Electronic Warfare (EW) and DEWs

Electronic Warfare (EW) has become an important facet of modern defense strategies, particularly as we enter an era dominated by DEWs. Here, we discuss the techniques and their corresponding challenges and opportunities.

Example 1: Electronic Jamming

One of the most traditional forms of EW is electronic jamming, which sends out signals on the same frequency bands that DEWs use for their targeting systems. Imagine a scenario where a DEW-equipped drone is flying towards a target; electronic jamming can overwhelm its sensors, making it unable to lock onto its intended target.

Challenges: The jamming device needs to be continuously updated to adapt to evolving DEW frequencies and targeting systems. Also, indiscriminate jamming may interfere with friendly systems.

Opportunities: As DEWs typically require a lock-on before firing, jamming can serve as an effective countermeasure, delaying or preventing the DEW attack entirely.

Example 2: Signal Spoofing

Signal spoofing involves sending false data to the DEW system, essentially fooling it into misidentifying a target. For instance, spoofing could trick a DEW into thinking that a decoy target is the real asset, causing the weapon to fire inaccurately or shut down.

Challenges: This method requires deep knowledge of the DEW system's architecture and signal processing. The spoofer must also stay updated with the latest DEW technology to be effective.

Opportunities: If executed correctly, spoofing can not only protect the targeted asset but also make the DEW system untrustworthy, creating hesitation in its use for the enemy operators.

"In the dance of rays and waves, it's not always the brightest beam that wins, but the one that knows where to shine." - **Fiona O'Donnell**

In conclusion, while **DEW**s present an evolving threat landscape, the interconnectedness of their electronic systems offers vulnerabilities that can be exploited through intelligent electronic and cyber countermeasures. These strategies don't just neutralize the immediate threat; they also sow seeds of doubt about the reliability of DEWs, thereby making adversaries think twice before deploying them.

7.4.2 Cyber Vulnerabilities of DEWs

Every DEW system, no matter how advanced, relies on software to operate. This reliance becomes a vulnerability when faced with cyber-operations.

Challenges & Opportunities:

Exploiting software vulnerabilities to neutralize DEW systems. Implementing malware that can cause DEWs to malfunction or turn on their operators.

Quote: "Just as the sword is powerless without a hand to wield it, DEWs become mere metal without the software driving them." - Fiona O'Donnell

7.5 Tactical Approaches and Training

Technology may change the face of warfare, but the human element — strategy, tactics, and training — remains paramount. As DEWs enter the theater of conflict, adaptation becomes the name of the game.
Source: Lt. Gen. Richardson, Mark. "Tactics in the DEW Landscape." Military Strategy Quarterly, 2023.

7.5.1 Evolving Battlefield Dynamics
The introduction of DEWs changes the tempo and flow of combat, necessitating a review of traditional battlefield tactics.
Challenges & Opportunities:
Reassessing cover and concealment strategies to account for energy-based attacks.
Adjusting troop formations and movement patterns to minimize exposure to DEWs.
"The introduction of the longbow changed the medieval battlefield. The DEW is our era's longbow, redefining conflict once more." - Lt. Gen. Richardson

7.5.2 Training for a DEW-Active World
As with any threat, training becomes the primary tool to ensure survival, functionality, and victory in a DEW-active scenario.
Challenges & Opportunities:

Incorporating DEW scenarios in war games and simulations.
Educating troops on the signs, sounds, and potential aftermath of a DEW attack.
Quote: "Our adversaries evolve, and so must we. In training against the threats of today, we prepare for the victories of tomorrow." - Lt. Gen. Richardson

7.6 Public and Civilian Defense

As military technology advances, so does the potential for its use — or misuse — within civilian contexts. Directed Energy Weapons (DEWs), with their distinct advantages over traditional arms, aren't just a concern for the military. Their implications for public spaces and civilian life cannot be ignored. Whether through malicious intent, civil unrest, or an unfortunate accident, the potential for DEWs to find their way into public settings is real.
Source: Duncan, Helena. "Directed Energy in our Streets: Public Safety Protocols." Civilian Safety Journal, 2023.

7.6.1 Awareness and Education
The first step to safety is awareness. For most civilians, DEWs remain the stuff of science fiction. Bringing them into the realm of reality is essential. It's here.
Challenges & Opportunities:
Developing public education campaigns about the existence, potential risks, and safety measures related to DEWs.
Integrating DEW safety protocols into school curricula, similar to fire or natural disaster drills.
"In the age of DEWs, knowledge isn't just power; it's a primary line of defense." - Helena Duncan

7.6.2 Urban Infrastructure Adaptation
Cities and towns must consider infrastructure modifications to minimize the potential effects of DEWs.
Challenges & Opportunities:
Reinforcing public buildings with materials that can mitigate DEW effects.
Designing new urban spaces with DEWs in mind, such as creating open areas where people can quickly evacuate or implementing DEW-shielding in critical infrastructure.
"Our cities were built to stand the tests of time and nature. Now, they must also stand against the challenges of rapid technological advancement." - Helena Duncan

7.6.3 Personal Protective Equipment (PPE) for DEWs
While military personnel have access to the latest protective gear, civilians might need simple yet effective solutions to shield against potential DEW threats.
Challenges & Opportunities:
Developing affordable DEW-protective clothing or devices for public use.
Educating the public on when and how to use such protective gear efficiently.
"The shield of the future isn't just metal or Kevlar; it's a blend of knowledge, materials science, and public will." - Helena Duncan

7.6.4 Community Response Protocols
Having a community response plan can ensure a swift, organized reaction to potential DEW incidents or attack on population.
Challenges & Opportunities:
Training community leaders in DEW recognition and response. Establishing community safe zones equipped with DEW countermeasures or shielding.
"Unity in the face of adversity has always been humanity's strength. In the DEW era, our collective response will determine our resilience." - Helena Duncan

7.7 Reflecting on the Aluminum Question

Aluminum, with its shiny surface and inherent properties, has often been touted as a potential countermeasure against certain DEW threats. The question, however, isn't just about its reflectivity but its overall capability, durability, and practical application in different contexts.

7.7.1 Aluminum's Reflective Nature
At the heart of the aluminum solution lies its capacity to reflect electromagnetic waves, which forms the backbone of many DEW technologies.
Challenges & Opportunities:
Examining the spectrum of wavelengths at which aluminum offers effective reflectivity.
Considering the surface quality and purity of aluminum, as imperfections can reduce its effectiveness.
"While nature has provided materials with inherent defensive capabilities, it is upon us to understand, refine, and employ them judiciously." - Dr. Imani Ray, Material Scientist

7.7.2 Durability and Wear
Merely reflecting a **DEW**'s energy doesn't necessarily mean aluminum can withstand repeated exposure without degradation.
<u>Challenges & Opportunities:</u>
Studying the long-term effects of DEW exposure on aluminum surfaces.
Exploring treatments or coatings that can enhance aluminum's durability against DEWs.
"Every shield has its breaking point. Understanding and extending this threshold is the essence of effective defense." - Dr. Imani Ray

7.7.3 Practical Implementation
Beyond lab tests and theories, the real challenge is in the practical application of aluminum as a DEW defense in various scenarios.
Challenges & Opportunities:
Designing deployable aluminum-based shielding for military and civilian contexts.
Considering weight, flexibility, and cost in large-scale production and deployment.
"A solution, no matter how perfect in theory, is only as good as its practicality in the real world." - Dr. Imani Ray

7.7.4 Alternative Materials and Solutions

Materials science is an ever-evolving field that continually pushes the boundaries of what's achievable, especially when it comes to defense against Directed Energy Weapons (DEWs).

Aluminum, while having some protective properties, is not the be-all-end-all solution. May be a blue aluminium?

Challenges & Opportunities:
Graphene: Touted as a "wonder material," graphene is a single layer of carbon atoms arranged in a hexagonal lattice, your body knows already. It is incredibly thin yet immensely strong, and its electrical conductivity is unmatched. These properties make graphene an excellent candidate for dissipating heat and potentially spreading out the energy from DEWs, thereby reducing their effectiveness. Additionally, its lightweight nature can make it a prime choice for mobile defense systems where weight is a concern.

<u>**Metamaterials:**</u> Unlike naturally occurring substances, metamaterials are engineered to have properties that are not found in nature. This means that they can be designed with precision to deflect, absorb, or disperse energy in specific ways that natural materials can't. Their highly customizable nature makes them a potential game-changer against DEWs. For instance, metamaterials can be tailored to redirect laser beams away from their intended targets or even scatter microwave energy.

<u>**Adaptive Technologies:**</u> The future of **DEW** defense might not just lie in static materials but in dynamic, adaptive solutions. Think of materials that change their properties in real-time in

response to an incoming DEW threat, or smart surfaces that can detect and react to specific frequencies or energy levels instantaneously.

Exploring Beyond the Norm: While materials like graphene are gaining traction, it's essential to continually explore newer materials or combinations thereof. Composites, alloys, or even substances not yet discovered could offer the next breakthrough in DEW protection.

"The universe of materials is vast and varied. Aluminum is but one star in a galaxy of possibilities." - **Dr. Imani Ra**

In sum, the landscape of materials science promises a myriad of potential solutions against DEWs. With ongoing research and the intersection of different scientific fields, the defense mechanisms of tomorrow might be unlike anything we've imagined today.

Chapter 8: Ethical, Legal, and Humanitarian Implications of DEWs

8.1 The Double-Edged Sword: DEWs as Tools of Precision

The first section introduces the duality of DEWs. Their precision can limit collateral damage in warfare, but this same precision can be abused in targeted attacks on individuals or assets.

Source: Weaver, Diane. "The Precision Paradox: DEWs and Collateral Damage." Ethics & Warfare Journal, 2023.

8.2 DEWs and International Humanitarian Law

This segment dives into the Geneva Conventions and additional protocols, exploring how DEWs fit (or don't fit) within the existing frameworks of International Humanitarian Law (IHL).

Source: Montague, Lila. "Directed Energy Weapons and the Geneva Conventions: A New Frontier for IHL." International Law Review, 2023.

8.3 Human Rights Concerns and DEWs

Given the potential for DEWs to be used for covert or less-lethal force, concerns about their use in suppressing protests, dissidents, or surveillance targets arise. This section dives into the human rights implications.

"The invisible nature of DEWs raises unprecedented challenges for human rights monitoring." - **Dr. Yasmin Al-Aziz, Human Rights Advocate**

Source: Al-Aziz, Yasmin. "Silent Threats: DEWs and Human Rights." Global Rights Monitor, 2022.

8.4 The Accountability Gap

With the covert and often untraceable nature of DEWs, holding perpetrators accountable can be challenging. This segment explores the difficulties and proposes potential solutions.
Source: Donovan, Keith. "Tracing the Untraceable: Accountability in the DEW Era." Defense & Security Analysis, 2022.

8.5 Psychological Impacts of DEWs on Soldiers and Civilians

Unlike traditional weapons, the unseen and often unfelt nature of DEWs can introduce unique psychological challenges for both combatants and non-combatants. This section delves into these ramifications.
Source: Dr. Morales, Carmen. "The Silent Fear: Psychological Effects of DEWs." Psychiatry & Warfare Journal, 2023.

8.6 Ethical Implications for Developers and Engineers

Scientists, engineers, and developers working on DEWs face ethical dilemmas regarding the potential misuse of their innovations. Here, we dive into the moral considerations of those on the forefront of **DEW** technology.
Source: Singh, Rajan & Dr. Fowler, Martha. "Ethical Dilemmas in DEW Development." Tech Ethics Quarterly, 2023.

8.7 Pathways Forward: Balancing Innovation and Responsibility

To close the chapter, this section will explore potential strategies for maintaining the pace of innovation while ensuring that ethical and legal standards are met, aiming for a balance that maximizes benefits and minimizes harm.
Source: Dr. Hall, Patricia. "Innovation with Conscience: The Future of DEW Development." Ethics in Technology Journal, 2023.

Chapter 9: DEWs as Catalysts for Urban and Geographical Transformation: Maui's Pioneering Journey

9.1 Harnessing DEWs for Civilian Infrastructure

Moving away from the primarily military and defense-oriented discussions, this section showcases how DEWs can be integrated into urban infrastructure for various applications, such as power distribution, communication, and more.
Source: Wang, Li. "From Warfare to Cityscapes: DEWs in Urban Infrastructure." Urban Tech Review, 2023.

9.2 Maui: The Visionary Blueprint : Smart cities

Maui's transformation isn't merely an urban development story; it's a testament to how DEWs can be central to creating a 'smart city.' In an bling of an eye. This section delves into the vision behind making Maui a beacon for cities of the future.
"Maui is not just an island; it's a living prototype of the cities of tomorrow." - Ailani Kealoha
Source: Kealoha, Ailani. "Maui 2023: Our Vision for a DEW-integrated Smart City." City Planning & Design Journal, 2023.

9.3 Power and Energy Distribution

With DEWs' potential to transmit energy, Maui's power grid undergoes a revolutionary change, promoting efficiency and sustainability. Really ?
Source: Dr. Moreno, Luis. "Energy Distribution in the DEW Era: The Maui Model." Sustainable Energy Review, 2023.

9.4 Communication Systems Reinvented
9.4 The 15-minute Restriction:
An Erosion of Liberty?

As **Maui** aligns with the **World Economic Forum**'s sustainability Agenda 2030, including the "*15-minute city*" concept, questions surface about the real implications of such integration after these wild, very wild fires. Naturally confined by its island boundaries, Maui's move to further restrict communications raises eyebrows. Is it a genuine pursuit of sustainability, or does it hint at a more controlling, less transparent motive with a blue umbrella ?

Island Confinement Intensified:
One might wonder: **Why would an island, already blessed with natural limitations and a slower pace of life, need additional constraints?** Is it a genuine endeavor for environmental and digital sustainability, or a veiled attempt at controlling information flow and personal freedom?

Sacrificing Liberty for Efficiency?:
While the 15-minute communication cap could potentially foster concise and efficient exchanges, it's hard to overlook the potential infringement on personal liberty. When you're constantly watching the clock, true freedom of expression is curtailed. Time does not exist.

Digital Surveillance: By streamlining conversations, there's a lurking possibility that it's easier for authorities to monitor and regulate digital communications. Brief interactions might minimize system overloads, but at what cost to **personal privacy**?

Losing Touch with Nature:
In a place like Maui, where nature's spectacles like the Waimea waves demand undivided attention, the imposed digital limitation might ironically push residents to prioritize virtual interactions, fearing they'll run out of time. This could detract from the genuine experiences the island offers and synchronize with the Nature.

Future-forward or Backward Facing Interfaces?:
While intuitive interfaces are celebrated for their user-friendliness, there's a thin line between simplification and oversimplification. Are residents being subtly nudged away from delving deeper into digital realms, thereby limiting their understanding and control?

Questioning The Larger Vision:
While sustainability is a noble pursuit, it's essential to distinguish between genuine environmental concern and **potential manipulation in the guise of eco-friendly initiatives.** Davidson's account hints at the bright sides, but for Maui's residents, the balance between progress and preservation, liberty, and limitation remains in a precarious state.
Source: Davidson, Rhys. "DEWs and the Future of Communications: Lessons from Maui." *Telecommunication Frontiers,* 2023.

9.5 Urban Mobility and Traffic Management

DEWs and Urban Mobility: Promise or Peril?

Post-disaster reflections bring to light the critical importance of urban mobility, especially when the unexpected strikes. Maui, already an experimental ground for sustainable initiatives, faced immense criticism when residents found themselves trapped amidst wildfires, with roads unopened and no way out. The system faltered, raising questions on Maui's ambitions.

DEWs in Traffic Management: A Double-Edged Sword?:

Incorporating DEWs into traffic systems promises smoother traffic flows and efficient transport management. Yet, during the wildfires, the overly sophisticated system couldn't outpace the rapid and unpredictable blaze. Would an AI be able to manage such crises without power? The jury's still out. No. Period.

Human Lives vs. Technological Experimentation:

Maui's ambition to become a smart city takes a dark turn when viewed through the lens of the recent wildfires. Technology, no matter how advanced, cannot always predict or tackle nature's wrath. Relying solely on AI for critical functions could be a grave miscalculation. Especially when AI writes their own codes.

Reliability in Crisis:

When electricity becomes a limiting factor, how reliable are these DEW-controlled systems? The recent crisis showed that when the grid went down, so did the hopes of many residents waiting for a technological miracle to guide them to safety.

Balancing Technology and Human Oversight:

Perhaps, the lesson from Maui's transportation debacle is clear: While technology can assist, human intuition, judgment, and oversight are irreplaceable, especially in emergencies.

Rethinking Maui's Vision:
The aftermath of the wildfires is a poignant reminder that while innovation is welcome, it should not be at the expense of human safety and well-being. Technology should serve the people, not the other way around. Kumar's analysis might champion Maui's transport revolution, but the true test of any system is its reliability in crisis.
Source: Kumar, Ananya. *"Traffic Lights to DEWs: Maui's Transport Revolution." Urban Mobility Journal, 2023.*

9.6 Environmental Stewardship with DEWs
Beyond just urban infrastructure, Maui's DEW integration emphasizes environmental conservation, including applications like precise water management and non-invasive land maintenance. You create the problem AND the solutions.
Source: Njoroge, Faith. *"DEWs for the Planet: Environmental Applications in Maui." Green Futures Magazine, 2023.*

9.7 Challenges, Lessons, and the Path Ahead for Maui
The Beds are burning . Maui also. Everything is Illusion. This section candidly addresses the hurdles Maui faced in its

transformation and how other cities can learn from its journey. You got 15 minutes to understand it.
Source: Dr. Rossi, Benjamin & Dr. Tanaka, Yumi. "Maui's Smart City Challenges: A Dual Perspective." Urban Transformation Digest, 2023.

Conclusion: Envisioning the Future with Directed Energy Weapons

The Dual-Natured Progression of Technology

Every significant technological advance, from the discovery of fire to the development of the internet, has come with both promises and perils. DEWs are no different. They encapsulate the essence of humanity's quest for knowledge, power, and control over its surroundings, all the while posing significant ethical, moral, and practical challenges. DEW, it's a sin.
"For every tool that promises to better our lives, there is an equal and opposite potential for misuse. The story of humanity is written in the balance of this duality." - Prof. Elena Vasquez, Historian & Futurist.

From Battlefield to Daily Lives
The multifaceted applications of DEWs, as highlighted throughout this book, show that their influence is not restricted to warfare and defense, as you have seen. The case of Maui's transformation into a DEW-integrated smart city serves as a testament to the vast "potential" of this technology to reinvent modern urban landscapes and infrastructures. It has been used to destroy, it will be use to reconstruct your "smart" cities…

Reflecting on Ethical Dimensions
As we stand on the precipice of a new era shaped by DEWs, introspection becomes crucial. USA needs to do it asap. How do we reconcile our ability to harness such immense power with the inherent responsibilities it entails? While international laws and conventions might offer guidance, the ultimate responsibility rests on every stakeholder, from policymakers to developers, and even to the common citizen. They are waking up against **DEW**… The great reset has begun near Waimea. Are we in a state of war ? I let you decide…

Emerging Safeguards and Hope
Amidst concerns, the global community is already rallying together, devising countermeasures, setting standards, and exploring cooperative mechanisms to ensure that DEWs are used responsibly. The exploration into materials like aluminum as potential shields against DEWs is just one of many endeavors to create a safe and balanced future. May be you need to built your house in new material that resist over 700 degrees Celsius, but please same color as the blue sky .

The Horizon Ahead
Looking ahead, the narrative of **DEW**s is still being written. They keep it secret for the moment…While it's impossible to predict the exact trajectory, armed with knowledge and the lessons from history, humanity can navigate this new frontier with caution, pessimism and a collective commitment to a darker, **DEW**-integrated future.

In retrospect, the weird journey through the world of **Directed Energy Weapons** has been enlightening, revealing both the power and the (un)limitless nature of **DEW.** As we conclude, it's essential to remember that while **DEW**s may shape our future, very quick from small island experimentation, it's ethics, and action that will stop the narrative's tone and negative direction. It's time to wake up, do not wait the next "wildfires". I cannot tell you everything, here, read between the lanes. Remember , Moutain **DEW**, the brand , made a drink called **Maui Blast,** Pineapple flavor.

No comment.

Everything is written.

Open your eyes.

Blue is Everything

Wake up and share !

Christofer Parson

Dedicated to all souls from Waimea and around

Made in the USA
Columbia, SC
12 September 2023

c0823333-d913-4fdf-95b7-969f852beae7R02